HEAVEN

An excerpt from

Climbing the Mountain

Direction for Our Times
as given to Anne, a lay apostle

HEAVEN

An excerpt from
Climbing the Mountain

Direction for Our Times
As given to Anne, a lay apostle

ISBN: 978-1-940737-30-0
Library of Congress Number: applied for

Publisher: Direction for Our Times

In Ireland:
Direction for Our Times
Tearmann Anama
*Headquarters of the Apostolate
of the Returning King*
Ballyjamesduff
Co. Cavan
Ireland
+353-(0)49-437-3040

In the USA:
Direction for Our Times
West 81st Street
9000 West 81st Street
Justice, IL 60458
USA
708-496-9300

Paintings of Jesus Christ the Returning King
and Our Lady Queen of the Church by Janusz Antosz.

www.directionforourtimes.org

Imprimatur

Nihil Obstat: Very Rev. John Canon Murphy, PP, VF

Imprimatur: ✠ Most Rev. Leo O'Reilly,
Bishop of Kilmore, Ireland.

Contents

Dear Reader,

I am a wife, mother of six, and a Secular Franciscan.

At the age of twenty, I was divorced for serious reasons and with pastoral support in this decision. In my mid-twenties I was a single parent, working and bringing up a daughter. As a daily Mass communicant, I saw my faith as sustaining and had begun a journey with Jesus, through my Catholic faith and the Secular Franciscan Order.

At the age of twenty-eight, I met a wonderful man. My first marriage had been annulled and we married and were blessed with an additional five children. Spiritually speaking, I had many experiences that included what I now know to be interior locutions. These moments were beautiful and the words still stand out firmly in my heart. I took it as a matter of course that Jesus had to work hard to sustain me as he had given me a lot to handle. In looking back, I see that he was preparing me to do his work.

During this time and after, I also began to experience locutions from the Blessed Mother, in addition to Jesus. Their voices are not hard to distinguish. I do not hear them in an auditory way, but in my soul. By this time I knew that something remarkable was occurring and Jesus told me that he had special work for me, over and above my primary vocation as wife and mother. He asked me to write the messages down and that he would arrange to have them published and disseminated.

All has happened as he said and I pray that we can all serve him according to his loving directions.

Yours sincerely,

Anne, a lay apostle

The Allegiance Prayer

Dear God in Heaven, I pledge my allegiance to You. I give You my life, my work and my heart. In turn, give me the grace of obeying Your every direction to the fullest possible extent. Amen.

The Vocation Prayer

Oh Mary, mother of Jesus and Queen of the Church, I ask you to bless me with fidelity to my vocation. Assist me in seeing that my service, however humble and hidden, is important to the universal Church. Strengthen me in times of trial and watch over my family and loved ones. Help me, beloved Mother, to remain faithful to Jesus Christ, your Son, the Returning King. Amen.

HEAVEN

An excerpt from
Climbing the Mountain

Direction for Our Times
as given to Anne, a lay apostle

August 28, 2005

Jesus said, *"You can see that I do not leave you, even for a moment. You should not fear this newest project because it will be similar to other experiences you have had. What will occur is this. I will take you mystically with Me for short periods of time. You will be aware in your senses, in as much as you will remain in your body. Your soul will accompany Me to heaven so that you can see what it is that I wish to show you. You will then record these experiences. My purpose in this is to reveal the truth to My apostles. Heaven is a truth. Souls serve Me on earth and they will then join Me in heaven. I am giving souls great courage through this grace. You need not worry over the publication of this work, Anne. That is My problem. I will reveal exactly how I wish these words to be disseminated. This project will be completed by mid-September. You will experience these visions with My constant companionship and you can talk to Me throughout and ask Me questions throughout, as you did today. Now, with the greatest trust and courage, record the small taste you were given today."*

I will try. Jesus drew me away from the crucifix, where I gazed, transfixed. He said, *"Leave My Passion for a moment and come with Me to heaven."* I did, and felt a sleepy kind of calm. I closed my eyes and rested in this calm and let Jesus' voice draw me away with Him. I was apprehensive in the beginning because Jesus had told me during Communion that this would occur. I began to see a vast area. There were distinct places but I got the strong and repetitive impression of no separations. I thought of a coliseum because these were places where great numbers gathered but there were no walls. It was like a middle place was raised. Jesus said:

"Souls who served together on earth, or who served in the same fashion, take the greatest pleasure in assembling for festivals or on feast days. There are many places for these gatherings. Let us join one."

We came closer and I could see a great number of souls sitting around a raised dais. I knew immediately that this was the gathering place of Franciscans. I thought I would see Saint Francis in the middle, speaking, because someone was there, but as we came closer it became clear that it was a woman. She was dressed like a queen except not showy. She wore a gown with terrific light movement. She was beautiful but I cannot describe her. She looked young and joyful and wore something on her head, a small crown that, while understated, was of the greatest quality. She was speaking to those gathered around. I said, "Jesus, who is it?"

"It is Clare," answered Our Lord.

She glanced at me and smiled and said, *"We have a visitor."*
I called out for Jesus and He began to speak again. He said,

"Look at this audience, Anne. They are all saints. Many served as Franciscans but there is no separation in heaven so all are welcome. Many like the concepts

being taught here so they bring others. There is constant joyous learning in heaven and such companionship provides the loveliest peace to others. Do not be afraid, Anne, because you are among friends. These souls know you and you will know them."

I was fearful again and I heard Saint Clare say, *"Let us take a moment and ask our Father to sustain little Anne so that she can persevere in His will."* I knew that this audience then grew silent and began to pray for me. I opened my spiritual eyes to look at the audience and saw two men in the front row. They had beards.

I said, "Lord, will souls have faces in heaven?"

Jesus was very patient and said, ***"You will know each other, yes."***

That is what He said. We then backed away from this gathering place and Jesus brought me gently back to the room.

August 31, 2005

Jesus said, *"Record your experience. I will help you."*

Jesus drew me into Him and I experienced peace. He then said, *"What do you see, Anne? Look around you."*

I saw trees. We were above an area of beautiful trees. As I looked down at them, our Lord encouraged me to look more closely. I did and saw a stream cut into the ground. It was the most beautiful, clear water, moving steadily over rocks and moving downhill in a gradual way. I saw a woman on the other side of the stream from us. She was sitting on a rock, looking at the water and listening. I approached her, on Jesus' urging, and she gave me the most beautiful smile.

She said, *"Listen, Anne. Listen to the sounds."* I did and the sound of the water was beautiful, like music. There was so much to it that it was like a symphony because there were so many different aspects of the sound. I had to settle in on small parts at a time. The music in a symphony blends together and you hear it as a whole. That stated, intellectually you understand that much has gone into the music's preparation and so many instruments come together and blend for the finished music. This stream was similar in that way.

Jesus said, *"You see that this saint is learning about Me from listening to the sounds of the stream. I created water, in its purity. She is contemplating My goodness in giving so many gifts to souls on earth. She is contemplating the depth of My wisdom as the Creator. She is learning about purity, about love, about the movement of the Spirit through all things created. Anne, this is how holy souls are on earth. When they contemplate the beauty of nature, they see Me. I am the Creator."*

I thought of my spiritual director looking at the sunset as our airplane approached Chicago. He was awed by the majesty of it and said, "Imagine people trying to say God does not exist."

I asked Jesus if we would be eating in heaven. I realize how that sounds but I was curious. He said that we would not experience a compelling need to satisfy an urge. We would have different kinds of bodies in that we will not have to be slaves to our bodies as we are here. We will have feasting, but not in the same way. When I looked at the water, I wanted to drink it. He said that I will be able to taste things in heaven. When I was initially looking at the scene of the stream and the woman, He told me to listen.

He said, *"You have your senses, Anne. Listen to the beautiful sounds."*

I want to convey to souls how delighted Jesus was to be giving me this experience. He was so happy at my innocence in surveying the heavenly Kingdom. He was so happy at my happiness. This is how Jesus will be for us all. He will introduce us to the heavenly Kingdom personally. He is totally available to me during this time for any silly questions I have or any observations. This woman, Mary, an unknown saint, told me some personal things and asked me not to be afraid. Jesus then drew me away and brought me further up the stream, and up, and up higher to the spot where the stream originated. It came out of a mountain and appeared quite unimpressive at its source. But from this small flow bubbling from the ground had come an elaborate run of water, growth, sound, beauty, and grace. The land near the stream, all down its length, was bordered by flowers and trees and all created things.

I asked Jesus if there were fish in the stream. He said, *"Of course."*

I asked Him if we would eat the fish.

He said, *"No. You will not need to eat the fish."*

He was very patient and gentle. I want to say He was slightly amused at my questions but in the kindest way. I felt like a four-year-old who is completely safe and cherished and knows only total security. I love Him so much and everyone else will too.

He brought me up to very high ground and I could see mountains and valleys stretching as far as forever. There was no feeling of being hemmed in or crowded. I did not see any other souls but Mary. This indicates to me that there is total isolation if you desire it and complete companionship as well. I imagine I will go from one to the other as the alone time is spent with the availability of Jesus. I should remark that one of my impressions is that this heaven is very like all that is good on earth. We will be totally at home there. It is home. The nicest part of this all is Jesus. He bowls me over and I want to do anything for Him.

September 1, 2005

Jesus brought me with Him again. We moved over the area from yesterday and continued on past a range of mountains, the same ones I saw before. We moved swiftly and came down in what struck me as a city, but with no cars. I was aware of people, but not crowds. There was a square with something in the middle and beautiful pavement like cobblestones only bigger and intricately laid with perfection. There was a woman in the first floor window, holding a cloth in her hand. She was waiting for me. It was nicely warm or comfortable in temperature. There was no window, now that I think about it, just the opening in a beautiful stone building. There was no risk of anyone falling out, I guess, because it was the first floor and you would see at least glass on earth. I seem to get stuck on these details. I got an impression of who this was but said, "Jesus, who is this woman?"

He said, **"She is another Anne. You know her."**

I looked again and she was looking at me intently. This was my father's mother, my grandmother. I never knew her. She died before I was born. I pray for her every day though, and have had several strong experiences of her. She was a special woman, I know. She spoke to me and encouraged me. I was not listening very carefully and had looked away.

When I glanced back she met my gaze with the most piercing eyes and said, *"Don't be afraid. Your spiritual senses are not developed and that is why you are distracted. We are all here but we are also with you."*

Jesus said, **"Our little Anne is struggling today so we must all pray for her."** There were other people in the room with her and I wondered why they were together because I knew them. They were all so happy. My grandmother gave the appearance of energy and business.

I said, "What are you doing in there?"

She replied, "I am organizing. I like to organize things."

I said, "Are things disorganized in heaven?"

They all laughed. She said kindly, *"No. Things are beautifully organized in heaven. But sometimes I like to reorganize them because it makes me happy. Anne, you will be very happy here. You are like me and you like to be busy. I would not be happy if I had nothing to do so I keep busy in doing things that create order in the way I envision order. You are creative. Your creativity will give you even greater joy here than it does on earth."*

We began to move away. Like yesterday, I did not feel any sadness on leaving these souls because I know that I am not. In a strange way, they are coming with me and I am remaining with them. I understand clearly that there is no separation between heaven and earth. I must remark that she was with people I know, but people she could not have known on earth. She, my grandmother, explained that they will be together during periods by choice to greet me or meet me or sustain me. The camaraderie between the souls in heaven and the souls on earth cannot be stressed enough. We do not have the divine vision yet, but they sure do and they use it to help us in everything.

From here, Jesus took me away. I looked down and saw a park. In the middle was a fountain. I had the impression of a Japanese style of garden in one area, so beautiful and orderly and gentle. Of course, I put my hand in the fountain and became enthralled by the movement of the water. Water seems special in heaven but I understand that it is my enhanced perception that makes it special. There is the beautiful noise of it, the movement, and today, the play of light in the droplets enthralled me. Jesus allowed me to rest here. I am like the child who comes into a play room, filled with the most elaborate and magnificent toys, but who begins to play with the springy door stopper. The parent, in all frustration, tries to draw the toddler's attention to the magnificent toys but all the child wants to do is bounce the spring to hear the lovely ping noise. Only Jesus, unlike an earthly parent, understands that it is a lot to take in so He lets me rest by the fountain. He then shows me the scope of these gardens. This is a gardener's paradise and my sister will love it. Jesus shows me a beautiful bush. This has special meaning as I left some of these when we moved and I grieved for these silly bushes. No doubt that is why He has shown them to me. The gardens seem to go on forever. I am drawn away, back to the room.

"Anne, you are doing fine. It is not an easy thing to experience heaven while you remain on earth. At the same time, you can see that many of the things in heaven are similar to the things on earth in as much as these are created by Me to give joy to My children. You did not note the most important observation that you made to Me on your return to your chair. You said, 'Jesus, it is really all about love, isn't it?' And the answer is yes. It is all about love. My love for My children, My desire to please them and reward them, and the way My love flows through souls into each other. When you see love on earth, you know that I am present. Be at peace. This heaven has been created for all of God's children and all will be welcomed. The only souls who will not come to heaven are those who refuse My invitation. There is no need to worry over loved ones. They are given the choice

to make and most choose Me. But I need My beloved apostles to work hard during this time. Bring souls to Me while they are on earth. This is the best way. Bring My love to others and I can heal them and prepare them for heaven."

I want to add that yesterday, after I came back, I asked Jesus if we could swim in heaven.

He said, *"Of course you can swim."*

I would love to swim really far without a fear of drowning. I am not particularly buoyant here on earth and it takes great effort to stay afloat in the water. This has never stopped me from water sports, but it certainly has made them more challenging. So I will swim like a fish in heaven. Something else that I forgot to record is that Jesus told me on the first day that I would see family members in heaven, and people I know. I did not imagine that they would speak to me.

September 2, 2005

Today I walked with Jesus through a forest. The path beneath us was some kind of stone, smooth and worn and expensive looking. I can't describe it. Big warm stones, very smooth. There were trees around us and above them sunshine. The light was coming through the branches.

Jesus said, *"Look at the sunlight, Anne."*

I looked up, hesitating. I have a light sensitivity and would not look at any bright light without good sunglasses.

He said, *"It does not hurt your eyes. All of your physical infirmity is gone. Walk with Me in peace today and we will talk."*

I know I was surrounded by beauty but what interested me most was His presence and being with Him.

"Each soul on earth has a path that has been traced out for him. His culture, his parents, his placement in time, all of these things have been designed by Me. There are no separations in heaven so cultures and religions blend freely. You have seen the vastness of heaven, Anne, and yet you have seen only the smallest area. There is room for each soul and the reward for each soul has been prepared by Me."

I, of course, had the impression of an ant so I asked if there were animals.

"Yes. There are all things created here but there is no enmity between the creatures of God."

I said, "There is no hunting and no prey?"

He said, *"No. There is nothing like that."*

He said, *"Consider for a moment that you are finished on earth and that I have brought you here for eternity. How do you feel?"*

I considered that. I felt removed from earth but I did remember it and recalled so much pain. I said, "Lord, it was so hard. I would not want to do it again."

He replied, *"Look with Me, Anne. Look down at your suffering and see what I see. You can feel My love for you and even while you were on earth you felt My love. Look at one period of your suffering."*

I did and saw myself after a serious health problem. I had three children, and I was expecting a fourth. I was mostly on bed rest and could not manage the housework and the babies. It was a dreadfully difficult time. I winced, thinking of it and seeing myself in it, but I began to hear the prayers that were coming from me. This is what our Lord was experiencing. I heard things like, "I offer this for You, Jesus. Help me, Jesus. I trust You, Jesus. Strengthen my husband, Lord. Stay with us, Jesus. Make me better, Lord. Bless these people who have to help us, Jesus." I saw our Rosaries being said with extended families. I heard so many prayers of suffering throughout the nights. I am writing this back on earth now and see what He is getting at.

During that period, I did not feel Christ as I do now. On the contrary, He seemed like He was gone if He had ever been there at all. This was a period of great suffering. The experience Jesus had in this period was the opposite of mine. He watched a soul carrying a great cross, who offered it all to Him. With this commitment, He built a fortress in my soul that He could occupy. This was one dark night for me but Jesus drew the greatest consolation from it. He blessed the souls who helped us. He blessed us. He blessed our children. From the heavenly perspective, great things were happening during this time. Standing next to Jesus looking at it, I was so grateful that I prayed and remembered Him in my suffering. The grace, while invisible and indiscernible to us, surrounded us. I can see that from here. I sure did not see it when I was in it, but I did believe it and I, in faith, knew that Jesus had not abandoned us. I knew Our Lady had not abandoned us. There was great peace in that house, I can see from here.

"You see the struggling, Anne. Talk about the struggles."

I was going to say that I could also see the enemy attempting to persuade us that we were being ill-used by heaven. We were good, so why did we have what appeared to be such bad luck and so many crosses? The enemy constantly tried to destroy my peace by showing me that others had it easy and were blessed with health and money and vacations. I see that I struggled continually to align my view to heaven's vision and made acts of love to Jesus in the face of these temptations toward bitterness. During this time I felt so sorry for my husband, that he was so heavily burdened. From here, I see that Jesus was making him a saint. This was part of my husband's process. My acceptance of the suffering obtained peace for him. But there was struggle.

"And from the struggle, Anne, came great holiness. Talk about My great peace in the face of your struggles."

Jesus is not shaken by the struggles. Even my bouts of anger at Him for my suffering do not upset Him. I bring my anger to Him and He takes it calmly, like the best life coach in the world. He understands that my view is necessarily limited and that my anger at Him is part of my process of acceptance of the cross. It occurs to me at this moment that

Jesus is trying to make us all saints. I am looking down at the process. I am not upset by my failures because I see them as my pain and my struggle. I am rather pleased that at least I gave Him some kind of return on His great love.

"That is it, Anne. It is this I want others to see. They will not avoid the cross on earth. If they accept the crosses in their lives, I can make them saints. Holiness is a process and suffering is part of that process. It is all about service to heaven, in suffering or in an absence of suffering. Talk about My acceptance."

If a soul walked away with one thing from this, I, Anne, would like it to be peace. Jesus loves us each. I feel total acceptance from Him. He is calm and kind. The word tolerant could be defined as "Jesus Christ." He is all love. I feel that I will view things differently from this experience. That does not mean I will be casual about my service to Him because He is easygoing. It means I will walk with yet a deeper awareness of His involvement in each moment of my day. He is my Friend. He is your Friend. Each sigh, each prayer sent up in darkness with almost no hope, is heard by Him and He is interacting constantly in each moment of your day to give you exactly what you need to continue in spiritual growth. It will end, this life, and you will be so glad you gave Him each bit of fidelity and love. I see that my prayers were that much more powerful because of the darkness from which they burst from me. Praise God. We should strive for great acceptance in all because it is all from His hand and He never averts His gaze from us.

September 5, 2005

Jesus said, *"Record what you saw and heard, Anne. Do not be afraid. Simply speak the truth, as you know it, and I will help you."*

Our Lord took me back through the Valley of Solitude, where I initially met Mary, an unknown saint. He brought me up to the mountain range that borders this vast area and told me to look. I did, and became aware of many souls, sitting alone. From my vantage point, initially what I noted were the beautiful trees and growth, the slopes of the land, the rivers and streams. It was only after He called my attention to these individuals that I became aware of them. They seem to take up no space at all. I asked, "Is this called the Valley of Solitude?" I was already wondering how I would convey this to others.

He said, *"It is a valley of solitude. But it is only one of many. These are places where souls come to converse with Me in privacy and silence. They learn about Me and come to know Me better. As you know, there is no separation from Me here. But in these areas souls enjoy complete solitude, within which they can absorb more, and then more again."*

I understood and we moved on. Jesus brought me on past the city where I had stopped and spoken. I asked Him how souls moved here.

"Souls move at will," He replied.

Well, it certainly seems that way to me as my soul moves

freely. I think we must move at His will because when He starts to move I move with Him. I guess that is obvious, given that we are in heaven and it is all His perfect will. We stopped at another building.

I was having trouble and He said, *"Anne, you are a child of God. You have every right to be here. Look, Anne. Look inside. What do you see?"*

Well, I saw a table, a beautiful table in a room that seemed to be a kitchen, except I did not see a stove. The table was wood and I was aware that there were men sitting around it. I did not look at them, as I could not bring myself to do so. Jesus told me to listen to them and I did. They were discussing events in the world. They were strategizing, it seemed to me. The theme or the general challenge being discussed was how they were going to bring the greatest number of souls to safety. I want to say that the threat to souls is from the evil in the world, not God's purifying events.

One man addressed me directly and welcomed me. He spoke and I knew him to have spoken to me before. He was Saint John of the Cross. He talked about the times. He told me that they were all there to help and that I was one part of a team. He directed me to the man at the head of the table. He told me that this was Saint Peter.

Saint Peter began to speak and I listened carefully. I was very aware that they did not budge when Christ entered.

Jesus said, *"Remember that I told you that there are no separations here. They are always united to Me so My entering the room does not startle them. You are the visitor, little Anne, and you can see that you are most welcome in this room."*

I asked Saint Peter if these times were darker than the times in which he lived. He said this:

"In my time men worshipped false gods. There was self-will, of course, and sin. The difference between my time and your time, though, is the level of arrogance. Man thinks he is a god. Man is filled with arrogance. The great learning and knowledge is generally not being used to further each other, but to advance self. This is not the way our Lord intended man to live. Changes are coming, Anne, which is why you are here."

I asked him how I was supposed to speak to souls who were not Catholic. I get challenged to speak in a general Christian way, in order to touch more souls. Peter was very clear to me. "You are a Catholic, Anne. You speak as a Catholic and souls will be drawn to Christ. You must preach what you are and what Christ has made you. The Catholic Church holds the deposit of our faith on earth, the truths. You must defend this. Souls who hear you will recognize the truth and they will recognize Christ. Fear no man. We are always close to God's apostles on earth and we will help each soul to represent Him. The renewal has begun. All must work."

I listened, aware that I was like the smallest child in this room, like a four-year-old in a room full of adults. I was comfortable with my smallness. Indeed, I felt safe in my humility because these men were also humble. That stated, they were making plans that would impact millions of God's children. Jesus trusted these men implicitly and relied on them to influence us and to support us. It appears that Jesus has no need to micromanage. He loves. Men and women work.

Saint Peter directed my attention to the other end of the table and it was John the Apostle. I rested in his great love and innocence, just staring at him. He then directed me to Saint Barnabas, who sat across from Saint John of the

Cross. My impression of Barnabas was that he was the most agreeable and kind man.

The table was the most solid, durable piece of furniture I have ever seen. It was as smooth as glass, timeless in its strength and quality. Yet it was as simple a thing as I have ever encountered. I did not even notice the chairs or anything else. I kept my comfort by concentrating on the table. Peter continued to speak and told me to come to that room whenever I needed advice on the mission or advice for the apostles who were working on special projects for the mission.

He said, *"You are welcome here, Anne. We will direct you. When you are at a loss for words, come to John."*

He indicated Saint John of the Cross, of whom I know nothing. I was fearful at a speaking event once and Jesus told me that He was bringing me Saint John of the Cross, who would speak through me. This worked well as I was never at a loss for words.

"We will help you in everything," Saint Peter continued. *"You must be calm and work steadily, remaining in obedience. It will all work out."*

Jesus drew me away. I was left back in my room.

September 5, 2005

Blessed Mother

"Simply write what you saw and heard, Anne. I will help you."

Our Lady came and asked me if I would like to go with her. I was upset because of something that occurred right before and I asked for Jesus.

She said, *"I will take you to Jesus."*

She did but Jesus did not move to accompany us. He smiled and I felt more comfortable. Our Lady brought me through the places I had seen before. She stopped at the house in which the men sit around a wood table. I looked at their faces and they were filled with compassion.

She said, *"Many spoke badly about these people also, Anne. They understand. You will find great understanding in this room."*

We moved on and went to a place that was filled with flowers. There were groves and groves of flowers, all different kinds. We began to walk through the fields and Our Lady spoke.

"I am sorry that this hurts you, Anne. It is for this reason that I brought you here today. I knew you would be happy here. These gardens are filled with souls who were devoted to me during their time on earth. Each year, on the Feast of the Assumption, there is a festival and that is one of

the occasions when all of these flowers are arranged for a feast. I promised you I would bring you here and I always keep my promises."

It was at least a year ago that Our Lady asked me if I would like her to show me where they grew flowers for the Feast of the Assumption.

I saw white roses, peonies, lilacs in the distance, all kinds of delicate white flowers, some like baby's breath, some like little blue bells. The groves or gardens stretched as far as I could see and she smiled at me.

"Jesus is very generous to me, Anne. He is generous to all souls, of course, but He grants me great favors for my children."

I had the impression of souls around me, people, tending to bushes and beds. My heart was heavy and I had difficulty experiencing the joy. It would come to me in waves of happiness, to be with her, and walking with her, but then I would remember this hurtful thing.

"Anne, there will be those who seek to hurt you.
Look at how they treat me."

Well, then I began to cry, right there on the path. The thought that anyone would hurt her just undid me. She started to speak. She consoled me so tenderly that I felt happy and joyful. My peace was restored and I was able to enjoy the gardens again. Our Lady began to speak.

"It is not possible for heaven to insulate apostles from all

hurt, nor would we wish to. Anne, you have seen heaven. You have experienced the peace and the love, the quiet contentment, the laughter and the happiness. Heaven is the home that each of our little children longs for. There is no substitute that will grant the security offered by the family of God. Dear apostles, if you are misunderstood on earth, rejoice. You will be understood in heaven. If you are hurt because of your work for Jesus on earth, rejoice, because in heaven you will be healed and ministered to with the greatest love. Anne, did you see one soul here who was grieving? Have you experienced anyone in pain or distress? This humble little work is about heaven, the destination of all just souls. Dearest little children, I beg you to treat each other with the love and respect that you will experience in the next life. Begin living like these saints while you are on earth and you will be brought directly here when it is time. You will not be sad that you offered Jesus your suffering. You will be grateful."

I am hesitant to describe how it felt to be consoled by Our Lady. I will not do it justice. She is the most merciful, and yet the most powerful woman I have ever met. You see that I fall miles short. Let me try again, calling on all of the saints. I would suffer for this mother. And I would do what I could to further her cause. Her cause is the cause of Christ, of course. To put it bluntly, I get the feeling there is a hard way and then there is Our Lady's way. She is the cushion that softens the fall. She is the one who walks you past your mistakes quickly, lest they discourage you. Our Lady will not fail us. She is too tenderhearted. I will be more devoted to her after this because of her kindness and understanding.

Again, I have to remark that being in heaven makes me feel like a four-year-old. They say that you have to be like a child to get into heaven. I believe it. There are no pompous or arrogant souls. No smugness or self-satisfied ones. The souls in heaven are filled with wisdom and kindness. And we are all going to heaven.[1] God is good.

---

1. Any soul who loves God will be welcomed in heaven. Clearly, if a soul rejects Christ he will not choose heaven.

September 6, 2005

Today our Lord brought me with Him again. Through the valley and over the mountain ridge and into the city. I saw the same flowers that both border the paths and flow down through the middle. There are no cars. I guess that is obvious but I noted it today especially because there are buildings and they are separated by roads or pathways.

Before this, as we were moving through the valley, our Lord asked me to stop and listen carefully. I did and heard crickets singing. Everything here seems to be consoling to me. I recently told a friend how badly I missed the sound of crickets singing. Well, I heard them in heaven so I will not spend any more time being sad about being away from this lovely noise.

I was brought to yet another building, through the open doorway and into a room in the front of the house. There were women gathered. I knew on the way that we were making our way to St. Anne, the mother of Mary, and our Lord's grandmother. I did not have the impression of an elderly woman. She was beautiful. I did not look closely at the other women because I had difficulty. St. Anne began to speak. She welcomed me and offered me some advice. She then spoke about friendships in heaven.

"We are loyal to each other here, and take the greatest interest in the intentions of our friends. I tell you this so that souls on earth will understand how we conduct ourselves in heaven. If I receive prayers from a soul on earth who is asking for help with one who has a drinking problem, I will

call on some of my friends here. I call on the friends who have the most experience in those situations. We will sometimes gather to pray for an intention. With regard to the apostolate our Lord has begun through you, it is good for all to know that we pray constantly for those who have answered 'yes.' When a lay apostle is embarking on a heavenly mission or project, he should call on us in a particular way. We have surrounded this mission with assistance and accompany each apostle on each errand."

I asked her if men and women mixed in heaven. There seems to be women with women and men with men. Nobody laughed today but today is a serious day.

"Yes, Anne. Men and women mix freely. Think of the group gathered with Clare. Think of the audience. There were men and women there together. We are just gathering with these friends at this moment. You have many women friends on earth and there are times when you find the company of women pleasing. There are other times when you prefer the company of men or like to be in a mixed gathering. It is the very same here. The only difference is that we seek only God's will. That is what we want. We want to help Jesus to further the Kingdom on earth so that souls can be brought to safety. Anne, many are at risk at this time. And it is for this reason that God is sending so many graces.

"For now, think about your best earthly friendships. Those friendships most closely reflect the relationships here in heaven. I want to convey to souls that in heaven we work together and draw on the experiences of many to assist us in answering the prayers of God's earthly children. As you gather in prayer on earth, so we gather in prayer here in heaven. We pray with you and for you."

I glanced around and saw that there were five other women

there. They were in various types of clothes and I thought that there were mixed periods in the room. I had the impression of different kinds of dress from different centuries, actually. Anyway, Jesus drew me away and we left. After this I rested with Jesus for a time, just thinking of it all and trying to take it in.

Jesus said, *"It is difficult to absorb when you are in pain, I know. Anne, your wounds will heal, as wounds do. They will disappear. But the graces obtained through your offering of your pain will not diminish. You will be in heaven and you will see the graces reflected in other souls who are here because of the generosity of those who suffered for them.*

"Be at peace, My beloved apostles. The pain you suffer on earth, be it physical or emotional, will be utilized. I use each little act of love, each little sacrifice. And when an apostle gives Me his day? Anne, I can do great things with such an offering. My beloved apostles who have been called from darkness during this time must serve in great courage and confidence. All that they suffer, all of their service, brings light into the world. I am pleased with such cooperation and prepare the reward for each apostle personally."

September 6, 2005

Jesus came for me and took me away with Him.

He said, *"Listen carefully to My voice and you will not be afraid. Let Me lead you and you will feel comfortable."*

What followed was the most lovely experience I have had yet. Jesus took me to the Valley of Solitude. We rested on the side of another stream and He told me to close my eyes. I heard birds and crickets. I heard an owl.

Jesus said, "Do you like owls, Anne?"

I said, "I guess they're okay, Lord. I don't know anything about owls. I don't like the thought of being in a dark forest at night and being afraid."

"Why would you be afraid?" He asked.

"Well, I don't like bugs and things or wild animals. Would I have to stay in the forest at night?"

Jesus then explained. *"There are souls who crave the soft darkness of the forest at night, Anne. They love the sounds, just as you love the sound of the crickets. So I provide these souls with exactly the peace they desire, in the darkness of the night forest. If you craved light, you would simply move to an area of the forest that was light. But there are many beautiful things about a heavenly forest at night."*

I thought about this and could see His point.

"Lord," I said, "that would be fine. I would like to be in the forest at night. But I do not want anything to crawl on me."

Jesus laughed loudly and so did I.

"I will not allow it, Anne. I promise."

I am afraid that I did not do justice to this night forest but I'm not sure that I can. It was the absence of light but not a total absence of light. There were soft shadows. The trees made the most beautiful noises as light breezes then heavier breezes blew through them. Sound is so sublime here. So beautiful. One could sit and listen for hours to the varying degrees of sound made by the winds blowing through the leaves. There were also many animal sounds, none of them ominous.

We moved on over the mountain ridge and through the city. Jesus said He wanted to take me to a special place. We rose up high, and higher up until the light began to change. It became a dark blue in some areas and darker again in others.

Jesus said, *"Look, Anne. What do you see?"*

I opened my eyes and I saw millions of stars against the night sky. We were up in them. Some were close and some were far. None were close enough to touch. It was beautiful and Jesus did not speak. Neither did I. I looked and looked, trying to get my fill. I craned my neck upwards and looked all around. It was wondrous. The most beautiful part, even of this, is the peace that flowed from Jesus into my soul. Jesus pointed down, slightly to the right. I saw the earth. It was beautiful.

"What do you see when you look at the earth, Lord?" I asked Him.

Jesus considered for a moment. *"I see hope, Anne. I see hope when I look at the world. I hear songs of praise and prayers of gratitude. My heart is moved to great mercy when I look at the world."*

I thought this was good, given all that has gone before and the need for this mission at all. This was a moment and trip for joy so I was not going to be the one to bring up the problems on the earth. Jesus was happy and so was I.

It was time to go and He told me that there was one small stop before we were to return. Back into the city, down a little side road, and into a door. A beautiful woman sat at the table, doing something with a bowl in front of her. It was Our Lady and I ran to her. She opened her arms and greeted me with such pleasure and love. Jesus, as always, was with us. But I sensed something different and it was this. Jesus was at home here, as He was at home on the earth. He began to tell me about this place. It was a humble kitchen with red flowers in a cup on the table. This was one of our Lord's homes while He lived on earth. St. Joseph was there but I did not speak to him.

Jesus said, *"Many souls on earth long for a place that feels like their home. Anne, they will find that place in heaven. They will be with their loved ones and they will be at home, more so than they were ever at home on earth. I understand this longing as I experienced it Myself. This was My home and I felt happy in it. I have it here. Each soul will have a place here that is their home. Souls should understand that when they are forced to leave a home, it is only temporary. They will find it as soon as they arrive in heaven and it will be a joyful place, with none of the pain of their earthly home."*

There was terrific peace in this little kitchen and I did not want to leave. I simply did not want to go. Yet it was time. I asked Our Lady if I could come back to her here when I arrived in heaven and help her with whatever she was doing in the bowl.

"Of course you can, little Anne. You can come right to me here and I will wait for you."

Promise secured, we left and Jesus brought me back to the room. I will be the only child in heaven, I'm afraid. Everyone else seems to be grown there, but I feel like the smallest of children.

Jesus said, ***"Anne, you will not be the only child-like soul in heaven, I assure you. You are experiencing heavenly love and it creates an innocence that cannot be mimicked on earth. Have no fears. You are exactly as you should be."***

September 7, 2005

Today Jesus took me back to the Valley of Solitude. I rested there with Him and listened to the sound of the water. It was easier to hear this time. He explained to me that there were different areas in heaven and that the city I had visited was very close to the Godhead. The souls in that city had served Jesus with distinction. He said that all souls would have access to that city and would come there at some time. I think that the Valley of Solitude is a place where souls come before they enter the city, to prepare themselves perhaps.

We went into the city and entered a house, down a hallway and to the left. It was a large room and I was aware of approximately twenty-five people sitting in a circle. A woman spoke and Jesus asked me to listen to her. She talked about the situation on earth and urged the others toward the recommendation of a certain course of action. A man presented a different perspective and they discussed the topic back and forth. Jesus listened carefully to all, as did the others.

Jesus began to explain to me.

"These men and women are My closest advisors. They have great wisdom and concern themselves with the affairs of the Church on earth. They are aware of each detail as holiness ebbs and flows in the world. I listen carefully to their counsel because I trust them. They love each other so there is no aggression in their discussion. You can see that they treat each other with perfect respect. They are discussing the purification today, which is why I brought you to them. I want you to understand that each detail has been planned, not only

by Me, but also by souls who love as I love, and who seek only the advancement of My will. So you see, Anne, while it may look as though I have abandoned man, the truth is that I have planned each day down to the greatest detail. Do not view events with earthly eyes. View events with the goals of heaven in your mind and you will understand that all has been considered for the preservation of souls. The world is truly in the hands of heaven."

I understand that Jesus does not want me to fall into the trap of blaming Him for the difficulties in the world. I did have trouble last night when I viewed so much suffering. It is important to understand that God is in charge.

Later, Jesus brought me back to the same room. The man was now talking and Jesus asked me to listen, as what he was saying was important and part of the reason that Jesus had brought me here. The man spoke of the loss of heavenly influence on souls in their youth. He said that heaven should no longer allow children to be poisoned by the erroneous beliefs of their parents. He also cited situations in schools that drew children toward the enemy. The woman across from him nodded in agreement. She seemed to be quite an authority in the room. The discussion involved our children.

I said, "Jesus, how will You fix this?"

"We will have to work through the parents, Anne," He replied. *"This is part of his argument for the course of action he favors."*

We left that area then and moved up into the dark blue of the sky, far up into the stars, where everything is far away and yet all seems close. It is a very big place, this universe.

September 7, 2005

Jesus brought me to the Valley of Solitude and we sat by the stream again. He talked about the mission and helped me to understand why He was giving this grace. He said that these glimpses into the heavenly Kingdom are intended to inspire man to service and to help us to reject the fleeting material things that the world offers. We are to understand that what will endure will be our service, our love, and our devotion to our duties. He said that these glimpses would result in conversions because of the graces attached. He will communicate with souls through this work so that they will have a greater mystical capacity than before.

There is a lot of what I see that I cannot attach words to so I leave it with the peace that comes from Christ. How do you describe total security and love? I guess you can say that it is the complete absence of anxiety. That would be one way but only a small facet.

Jesus took me across the city and into the sky. Instead of going up into the heavenly universe, we crossed this sky, which was that glorious mix of blues and darkish colors, until we came to a different day. It was light then and we crossed another valley and entered a different city. This city was bustling. I had the impression of many souls.

Jesus reminded me to open my eyes and I locked onto the first person I saw, an Asian man. He had a ready smile as he prepared some kind of conveyance. I did not have the eyes or understanding to grasp what he was doing but he was a dignified man and I loved him immediately. Everyone in heaven is beautiful. This feeling of camaraderie is instant and complete. He stood in front of a building on a street where there were many buildings. Jesus told me that we were going in. As we stepped in the door I saw that it was kind of a church. There was an atmosphere of the greatest reverence. I looked at the audience and they were enraptured by what was occurring in the front of the church. Their faces were lit with joy and they all sang in sweet and soft voices. I wonder if they were Catholics as it's hard to get this kind of singing from Catholics on earth. Jesus said they were from different religions. They were certainly from different races. There was a complete mix of skin colors and bone structures. All were beautiful. I really do not know sometimes if I am seeing souls or faces. When I concentrate I do see faces. At any rate, all had a radiant look of love in their eyes.

I searched for the object of this love and saw Our Lady at the front of the church. They were singing to her.

I said, "Jesus, help me to understand what they are saying." I could not get words, just harmonies. And the harmonies were glorious. I was then able to discern certain words, including the word Mother. These souls were learning about Mary. Again, I must note that nobody reacts when Jesus enters. He mystically never leaves them. I had the impression of Christmas here in this church. There was a sense of wonder and innocence that I associate with Christmas. The priest at the front of the church, if it was indeed a church, was leading the praise. I could not share in what they were witnessing and this saddened me. I wanted to see what they saw and experience what they were experiencing. But I am here on a guest pass so it is not time. Jesus conveys to me that I will do so in the future.

It seems that souls have limited experiences on earth. Some have never heard of Mary, as difficult as that is for me to imagine. These souls get to learn about her in heaven. I am filled with the depth of divine justice and benevolence.

Take a soul on earth who has not been exposed to any faith at all. He comes here to heaven and he is able to absorb the greatest mysteries of the Godhead and the Kingdom of the divine. We must never pity a soul who dies as a child or dies without having any depth of faith or knowledge of faith. If the soul chooses Christ, that soul will experience it all and learn it all. My attempt here is pitiful, I know. I trust the Spirit to bridge the chasm between the reality and my attempt to represent it.

We leave. Jesus brings me across the street or road and we enter another church. This is a building dedicated to Saint John of the Cross. There are souls looking at various elements of his life and teaching. They are learning about concepts that they were not familiar with from their lives on earth. Jesus talks about learning and how it continues in heaven. These souls do not look bored. As in the last building, they have faces filled with wonder and awe. There are groups together, with one soul indicating various elements to others. There are souls on their own, gazing in silence at those displays that are not available to me. This John must be something. But Jesus indicates to me that in each life there are moments of great value and dedication or triumph over self. These moments are preserved. There is no sense of sin here at all. There is no sense of anything but joy. I cannot convey this and it makes me sad because I want to do it justice for souls on earth.

This area, while not crowded, is a lot busier than the city across the blue/black universe. There are the same flowers and trees and again, the beautiful sounds. Outside there is lovely light and the sound of breezes. Inside this building, where souls are studying Saint John's spiritual triumphs, there is a delicate chime sounding. It is not one note but a lovely quiet melody made up of the most exquisite notes. It provides a background of serenity and adds to the wonder. You could really come here just to listen to this music. I am made aware that this city is made up of countless buildings like this. Jesus talks to me at length about learning and how it continues in heaven, giving great joy to souls.

We step out into the light. I see souls again together and alone, all looking peaceful and some chatting.

I am back to my room at home with the words wonder and awe on my lips.

September 8, 2005

Today Jesus brought me to sit with Him by the stream. We spoke for some time about my role in this mission. I have been struggling with some issues and Jesus explained how I am to conduct myself. I was able to ask Him many questions. Afterwards we moved along the same course as yesterday, out of the valley, past the mountains, over the city and across the star-filled bluish sky. We entered the city where it is a new day and stopped again in front of the building that reminded me of Christmas. We entered.

Today it was vast. Souls filled this area and it seemed like the greatest cathedral. Our Lady was in the middle. Jesus instructed me to listen carefully and I did. A man was singing to her, a solo, and all souls listened and enjoyed the beauty of this loving voice that sang as a gift to Our Lady. This man was not a famous singer on earth. He was an unknown saint, as are most saints. The voice carried through the cathedral with absolutely no unnatural vehicle. There were no microphones. I listened and was drawn into the beauty of his voice, the love in his song. I was keenly aware that all of the souls present were enjoying this voice in the same way. It was a gift to Our Lady but also a gift to us all.

After he finished his song Our Lady thanked him. I did not see him. Our Lady was different than everyone else in that her movements seemed natural to me. She was not ethereal. She seemed to move as I would expect a person to move. Is that saying that nobody else moves normally? I don't think so. I am just not aware of the way others move here, but I am aware that Mary moved naturally and I could see her arms moving. She held flowers in her hands. She had a veil on. It was white. Over the veil was a crown. In the middle of the crown was an exquisite blue stone that represented her maternity. Many other stones surrounded that one. She is as pure and lovely as it is possible to be. Jesus told me to look at her carefully so that I could describe her. I could see that she was very happy. Jesus told me to look carefully at the scene.

Our Lady was surrounded by flowers. Each flower was an offering from one of the souls here to see her and to greet her on her birthday. I recognized some of the flower varieties and saw white roses. I also saw lilacs. This next point is important. There were many souls present. Countless. But each soul communed with Our Lady as though he or she were the only one there. So their time at this event or celebration was together with other souls, but also in separate unity to Mary. They could talk to her and converse with her as they wished.

She turned and spoke to me directly and the festivities carried on. So she was not ignoring anyone else when she spoke to me, but our conversation was distinct to us. I hope I am clear. She told me that souls come to her all through this special day. I asked her if she was given gifts because I did not see any presents. She said no, that each soul there was her gift and she considered every soul in heaven a gift to her because she considers each her child. Jesus has given her many graces for souls and when the soul is in heaven, Our Lady looks at the soul and sees the mercy and generosity of Jesus in them. That is her gift and it will endure forever.

She explained that one of the special things that occurred on this day was that she granted great favors to souls, favors she obtained from Jesus. She said that Jesus is very generous on these special days, her birthday and feast days.

I was thinking that this is the day to ask for things and she read my thoughts.

"What does my little Anne want today?"

I thought fast because I realized I had a lot of people who would be grateful for a mention at this moment. I could not single anyone out. There were too many. So I asked her to grant the intentions of anyone who has ever asked me to pray for them. I held my breath, knowing this was big, but I have long since learned that when one is dealing with heaven it is best not to limit our requests.

She gave me the most beautiful, intimate smile, and all of the other festivities faded away. Her voice seemed to fill me and echo through me. *"I will give this to you, Anne. I will grant favors to all who seek your intercession, both now and in the future. This is a special day for me, both in heaven and on earth. Jesus will refuse me nothing."*

I have to make another point here. All of these souls are saints. They are the Church Triumphant. They are all there and they have all brought intentions. This is not a greedy thing. They lack nothing. They are in heaven. They are not asking for themselves. They are petitioning for souls on earth and attempting to impact what happens on earth. We have not been abandoned.

I think that too few are asking for graces in this time because there are enough graces for all good things. And yet we do not have all good things in the line of virtues and humanitarian relief. But we have a lot of good things in our world and we have the opportunity to obtain great changes in that heaven is prepared to give freely during this time of renewal. So we must begin asking. We should ask all the saints to intercede for us. Today I saw them doing it. They had all brought petitions regarding their loved ones as well as for heavenly projects on earth.

It was time to go and I leaned back into Jesus, who is always behind me. Often during these experiences I call out to Him and His voice answers immediately. When I leaned back into Him He surrounded me and I felt so safe. Heaven is all wonderful. Our Lady is the joy of all joys. But I have to state, and she would want me to do this, that Jesus is everything. He is everything. Nobody reacts when He enters, I say again, because He never leaves. They must all experience Him as I do and maybe that is why they do not react. I know there is no separation. Jesus is in everything and surrounds everything. I can't say enough about how kind He is and how loving. I find I have to give a deep sigh and stop trying.

He led me gently back into myself.

September 8, 2005

In response to my question, our Lord said, *"Write it exactly as you experienced it."*

Jesus brought me with Him, explaining that this would be a short experience. He asked me where I was, twice, I think to help me to be aware. I was over the valley that leads into the city. When we got there, we turned to the left, instead of going straight on, which would be toward the blue night sky with the stars. We traveled in that direction for a time and came to the end of the city. There was a divide of some sort that led to a structure that was huge. We entered and Jesus asked me what I saw, to prompt me to look.

I saw a lot of people gathered in a semi-circle. They were waiting to see God the Father. Jesus said it was important to understand that there is a distinction between Jesus and God the Father. Jesus reminded me that He had brought me to God the Father before. This is true. I had an experience of it many years ago. I was not as afraid after that because it was a beautiful experience.

Jesus brought me to Him and I felt His piercing gaze go through me. My first thought was that this was the One I pledged my allegiance to at the Consecration of the Mass for years. He had heard me for years. All of those prayers were in His eyes in some way. It's as if all of those prayers were with me at that moment. He had been listening. God is paying attention.

The second thought that went through my mind is that quite simply, this Man, this God, knows EVERYTHING. No point in trying to get out of anything here. God knows it all. There is nothing hidden from His gaze. He was serious, in the extreme. I felt no fear, only love.

He said this: *"You are cherished. You know that I cherish you as My beloved servant. Anne, just as I cherish you, I cherish each soul. Work for souls. It is for this reason you have been called."*

He returned His attention to whatever He was doing when Jesus brought me to Him and I backed into the warmth of Christ. I was a little shaken and Jesus spoke to me quietly. After a time I came back to myself.

When I did, I asked, "Jesus, I understand you and God. What is the Spirit?"

He reminded me of the Valley of Solitude. During one of these experiences I saw a bird flying high, drifting in a stream of wind. The bird did not move its wings. It just remained still and the wind held it high above the forest. I don't know how long I stared at it but I could not take my eyes from it.

Jesus said, *"It is the Spirit that held the bird aloft, Anne. The Spirit is what connects all goodness. It is the Spirit that bound you to the Father. The Spirit moved through you, prompting you to pledge your allegiance to the Father, and the Spirit has sustained you since your Baptism. The Spirit supports all. Souls must ask for this Spirit and welcome Him."*

I'm thinking that it is the Spirit that seems to highlight one sentence in the Bible when you are reading and it seems to hit you hard or when it illuminates you completely.

I have also found that the wind blowing through leaves and moving the trees holds me spellbound. That must be the Spirit too. I am very aware of this Spirit in my days.

September 9, 2005

This morning Jesus gave me the opportunity to ask Him questions. I did this for a long time. This conversation took place in the Valley of Solitude, by the stream, as usual. I was able to listen and rest and this was pleasant. I closed my eyes at one point and listened at length to the sound of the leaves. The wind is alive here and as I felt it on my face I was drawn back to a time in my life when I had a similar experience. I had closed my eyes at that time also, and felt a soft breeze on my face. At the time, I knew it was a heavenly presence. This was well before my conversion. I was young and at a difficult place in my life. But I knew that the caress on my face was not from earth and I was comforted by it. This felt the same. It is all love in heaven and even the breeze ministers to souls. Recently someone asked me what Jesus looked like. I was startled because I did not know. I don't think I really see Him. I was alert today, for this reason, and realized that I am not so much looking at Him as united to Him. Heaven is unity to Christ. He is with you completely and you do not want anything else.

After a time He drew me away. We went into the city and turned left toward God the Father. Instead of continuing on, we turned right shortly before we would get to that big structure. Jesus brought me to another large structure and I understood that we were visiting the Passion. I did not want to do this.

Jesus said, *"Unity is complete here, Anne. Souls often visit the times of My life on earth. They do this to enter into the mystery of what was accomplished by God during those years. Time is different here. You understand this. The life and accomplishments of each saint are commemorated. In the same way, My life and accomplishments are honored. A good friend seeks to understand the difficult times as well as the joyful times. My Passion is alive here so that souls can enter fully into the mystery of the Redemption. Remain with Me for this short time."*

I did. I saw Jesus in the Garden and I entered immediately into the suffering. I felt it as a dreadful anguish and revulsion. This went on later as Jesus was pushed and pulled, mocked, spit on. I saw Jesus being whipped. This is how I saw it. I had an awareness of Jesus during His Passion, from the Garden to His death. I am having the greatest difficulty because I truly do not want to revisit this. The awareness would pause on highlights, which were the scourging, the crowning, the horrific carrying of the cross, and the crucifixion. I had the most horrid view of His poor little legs, which trembled under the weight of His broken body. The only way to cope with these experiences is to focus in on small details and this is what I did. Hence the fixation on His poor little thighs and legs.

I cried out and said, "Jesus, is this happening now?"

His voice came within me. He said, *"No. I am here, Anne. I am not suffering in this way now. But My Passion is honored in heaven and souls come here to be with Me in a mystical way. It is important that souls know that the depth of My sacrifice can be understood in heaven. This is a part of union, Anne, and you will come to experience this more gradually."*

We left this area and I came back to myself, a little shaken. Part of the reason this shook me up is this: In this heavenly experience, there is perfect clarity of the innocence and goodness of Jesus. He is the Lamb, the spotless One. He is all Love, all Goodness. And He is being tortured. I mean the nicest adult on earth at this time is still culpable for something, I would think. But not Jesus. He did nothing but serve. And this is where it took Him. It is a good example, indeed the perfect example, of love and service to both humanity and to heaven. This awareness makes it even more excruciating for me because I am not a resident of heaven. If I were, I would not feel shaken up. I would be gaining in understanding and knowledge. I would be entering the depths of His Passion and growing in wisdom of the sacrifice. This experience brought me clearly to the understanding that my work on earth is not finished. If it were, I would be at peace in His suffering. As it stands, I have my own suffering yet to complete. When I have, and when I am fully purified, I will be able to gaze upon this Passion in heaven and not be filled with remorse, but with love and gratitude.

September 9, 2005

We went through heaven via the same route. I felt joy and freedom. The greatest joy is asking Jesus questions. We turned right sooner than the Passion and I saw yet another vast structure. Jesus told me that this was the house of the Resurrection. He asked me to describe what I saw.

I saw millions of souls in rapture. They were riveted to the raised area in the front. I saw Jesus there. He looked similar to the Divine Mercy image only real. His hair was dark brown, it seemed to me. He was beautiful. He was love. All souls looked on Him and I understood that they had completed the study of the Passion. These souls were enraptured. There was another area and I asked Jesus what was there. He explained that His tomb was there. As I understand it, you can revisit the whole experience. In looking at these souls I was struck that they were in complete communion with Jesus. They were in Easter Sunday joy. It also ran through my head that some of them were there for millions of years. That was the longest time I could humanly attach to it. They were not bored. They were in ecstasy. The term millions of years means nothing, of course. It's just my way of saying a really long time.

Jesus said, *"Anne, this is important. These souls have entered into the mystery of the Resurrection. The greatest understanding of man on earth cannot compare to the smallest kernel of understanding in heaven. With understanding comes joy and wonder and reverence. It is for this reason souls gaze so long upon the Risen Christ.*

I make all of this available in heaven and souls come here often. Souls are welcome to rest in any of the heavenly mysteries. All is understood here. All is accepted. All is just. Souls feel only peace."

HEAVEN SPEAKS TO THOSE WHO DO NOT KNOW JESUS

Direction for Our Times
as given to Anne, a lay apostle

December 21, 2006
Jesus

I am Jesus. I am God. I am complete in myself. I am present in your world and I am present in Heaven. You see, I am omnipresent. Even if you wish to, you cannot remove yourself from my presence on Earth. I created Earth. You might say the earth belongs to me. All on it are also my creation. You, dear beloved one, were created by me. Do I say that you belong to me? I say it in another way. I say, I 'want' you to belong to me. I want to possess your heart. Why do I use the word heart when truly it is your soul that I seek? I use the word heart because people characterize the heart as the place where people hold the love they possess. If you have love, people say you have it in your heart. The heart is known as the source of love and the receptacle of love, so I, Jesus, tell you that I want to possess your heart. When it is all simplified, as it should be, I am saying that I want you to love me. I love you. There is no problem there. I love you today and I will always love you. A difficulty we have is that you do not know me. The only way for me to teach you to love me is for me to reveal myself to you, to allow you to know me. For that reason, I come to you today. I reveal myself to you through these words and through the graces attached to them. If you read these words and sit in silence, you will begin to know me. If you begin to know me, truly, you will begin to love me. Forget anything that tempts you to move away from these words and graces. Rest. Be with me. Allow me to teach you about myself.

Jesus

In your world today, there are many claims of goodness. Some of these claims are true. Some of these claims are false. I, Jesus, am not present in lies. I do not rest in falseness. Truth has a pure feel to it and truth does not change. If you want to find truth, look back over time and see what claims of truth have persevered. What are the things that were true two thousand years ago? You will find them if you look to see what has persevered through the ages. Two thousand years ago, it was true that I came to bring salvation. Today, that is still true. I came then and I come today. I come for your salvation. I come so that you will be saved. I come so that where there is falseness, where you are being deceived, I will be present with my truth.

Two thousand years ago, there was evil in the world. Today, evil persists alongside good. Does this mean evil is good? Has truth changed? No. Just as truth never changes, so evil does not change. Evil simply changes its disguise. I, God, have not changed my character. When you first know someone, you know a few things about him. As you get to know someone better, you learn more. Over time and with consistent interaction, you begin to know someone well and you can then say that you understand that person.

I want you to understand me. I am truth. To know me, Jesus, you will have to know what is true and what is false. I will teach you this but it is not something that I can teach you all at once. Truth, in its great depth, must be absorbed gradually. For this reason, I invite you to keep company with me. If you do, I will teach you all you need to know to distinguish between the truth in your world and the deceit in your world. I will teach you to separate good from evil at a glance. I am the great Teacher, the Divine Teacher. With me comes the light necessary for instant instruction on any given topic. You may say, "Give it to me all at once, God. If you are who you say, you can do that."

You are correct. I could do that. Such is my power. But you, my friend, are not disposed to accept such an experience because my truth is all about love. Your little heart must be expanded first. We have to make room for all of this truth, which is filled with love. I want you to embark with me on a journey. Walk with me. Allow me to draw you into your soul, into the mystical nature of yourself. Come to me there so I can introduce you to the great truths about your family, the family of God. You will find such acceptance there. When you rest in my gaze in your soul, you will understand about love. You will, at the same time, understand about Heaven, your ultimate home. I am calling to you now and I know that you hear me. Come to me. Stay with me. Give me the briefest chance to reveal myself to you.

Jesus

As I draw you into the mystical nature of yourself, I draw you into My heart. My heart and your heart belong together. When you are with Me, you feel calm and accepted. You feel oneness with others because you experience community in your soul. If I am with each man as I am with you, then you are connected to each man through me. Do you begin to understand the family of God? I love every man created. I have a good plan for every man created. This is my truth and, as you recall, I can never be where there is deceit. If I have a good agenda for every man created, and I have a good agenda for you, you are safe with me and all mankind is safe with me. If connected to me, each person will serve his time on earth in mystical union with every other person and in mystical union with all of the saints in heaven. We are all connected. After this time of service, each man connected to me comes home to me and home to the family that loves him, awaits him, and welcomes him. There is no bad will on Heaven's side. There is only acceptance and truth. I have such hope for you, my friend. All of your gifts originate in God and are an outgrowth of God's goodness. If you learn to understand me, you will learn that I want to use your gifts to create harmony in your soul. When you use your gifts and energy for my purposes, you will benefit the whole world. It must be so because I have said it is so and I can speak only the truth. We are all connected. Would you like to benefit the world? Truly, you are capable of this and this is my plan for you.

I have so much to give to you in terms of knowledge and wisdom. Teamed with me, you will flourish and grow to heights you never dreamed possible. Rejoice. You are resting with God, the God of All. This God tells you today that you are loved and needed.

Jesus

Follow this path that springs up before you. Come to me. Turn in my direction and I will reveal this path that I want you to take. You will feel lightness in your spirit, a relief. You will feel calm. Inside there will quietly burst forth a bud of hope. This bud will blossom, have no fear. The hope you feel in your soul is nourished by the time you spend with me, seeking truth. I will see to it all. I need the smallest, even the most tremulous willingness. You are hesitant to believe in me. I know that. I understand everything that has gone before this moment in your life. Remember that I have all universal truth available to me. In that respect, am I not a valuable person for you to know? Could you admit that I am possibly the most valuable person you could ever know? If you knew of someone on earth who had all truth about everything, who understood the purest facts and possessed the cleanest, most pristine vision of reality imaginable, would you not seek out this person's company? If you were wise, you would do so. If you were a man who desired truth, you would do so. If you were weary of lies and falseness, you would do so. My friend, if you seek truth, you must come with me. If you seek acceptance, you must come to me. If you want to be loved, you must rest in my heart because it is the only place where you will find the perfect security you crave. I am with you. I will never leave you. You could not escape my presence, even if you wanted to. You may as well get to know me better so that you can decide whether you will reject me or accept me. This is the

ultimate choice that will be yours. Just as you cannot escape my presence, you cannot escape this choice. It is yours. I want you to consider your options.

Jesus

My friend, this is between you and me. By "this" I refer to both this conversation and your ultimate decision of whether to accept me or reject me. When you are asked to make an important decision on Earth, you consider your options. You take time and weigh both sides. Perhaps you waver between one course and another. I want you to consider both sides of this decision. If you accept me, you will have entry into the most loving and secure family of all. If you accept me, you will have security for the rest of your life in that I will lay out the course in front of you, guiding you, protecting you, and never leaving you. If you accept me, you will come to heaven in triumph, bringing with you the great benefits that your cooperation secured for your family. You will walk in truth and in calm. Your life on earth will not suddenly become easy, but it will be filled with God's peace and God's grace.

If you reject me, you will continue on, vulnerable to the deceit of my enemy. You will delude yourself at times, thinking that you are wise. Perhaps you will feel superior to many of your brothers and sisters, but I tell you today, in all of my truth, that the most humble one in heaven holds all of God's mysteries in his soul. You will not be privy to these mystical realities if you reject me. How could you be if you did not want to be?

I conclude with one of the greatest truths of all and that is that I do not force my children to choose me. I do not force humanity to work for Heaven. If I did, we would not have a family, but a master and his slaves. No. This is not for me and this is not for you. The heavenly kingdom would not be the heavenly kingdom if it were not filled with willing and beloved children. Everyone in Heaven works for each other in great joy. Everyone in Heaven works for our family members on Earth in great hope. As you read these words, there is great hope in heaven that you will choose me, Jesus Christ, and embark upon the journey to truth. It is here for you. I have truth and I have a course laid out for you that will bring you to this destination.

I love you. I will take care of you. Choose me and I will begin to reveal myself to you. You will know peace, my friend. You will know security. You will know joy for all eternity. This is your inheritance and I am your God. Allow nothing to divert you from the truth that I am Jesus Christ and I love you. I come today to announce myself to you and to save you. Come. Trust me. Be with me. I will protect you.

APPENDIX

The Five Spiritual Practices

As *Apostles of the Returning King,* we will adopt the following spiritual practices, as best we can:

1. *Daily Allegiance Prayer* and *Vocation Prayer,* plus a brief prayer for the Holy Father

2. *Eucharistic Adoration,* one hour per week

3. *Prayer Group Participation,* monthly, at which we pray the Luminous Mysteries of the Holy Rosary and read the Monthly Message

4. *Monthly Confession*

5. Further, we will follow the example of Jesus Christ as set out in the Holy Scripture, treating all others with His patience and kindness

Three Charisms of the Apostolate of the Returning King

✠ *Compassionate Listening*
✠ *Learning and Teaching the Catechism*
✠ *Promoting Unity in the Church*

The Allegiance Prayer

Dear God in Heaven, I pledge my allegiance to you. I give you my life, my work and my heart. In turn, give me the grace of obeying your every direction to the fullest possible extent. Amen.

The Vocation Prayer

Oh Mary, mother of Jesus and Queen of the Church, I ask you to bless me with fidelity to my vocation. Assist me in seeing that my service, however humble and hidden, is important to the universal Church. Strengthen me in times of trial and watch over my family and loved ones. Help me, beloved Mother, to remain faithful to Jesus Christ, your Son, the Returning King. Amen.

Promise to Lay Apostles

May 12, 2005

Jesus

Your message to souls remains constant. Welcome each soul to the rescue mission. You may assure each lay apostle that just as they concern themselves with my interests, I will concern myself with theirs. They will be placed in my Sacred Heart and I will defend and protect them. I will also pursue complete conversion of each of their loved ones. So you see, the souls who serve in this rescue mission as my beloved lay apostles will know peace. The world cannot make this promise as only heaven can bestow peace on a soul. This is truly heaven's mission and I call every one of heaven's children to assist me. You will be well rewarded, my dear ones.

For instructions on how to pray
The Rosary and The Divine Mercy Chaplet,
please visit our website:
www.directionforourtimes.org

The Volumes

as given to Anne, a lay apostle

Excerpts from The Volumes

Jesus Speaks to You

Booklet containing the messages taken from
Volume Four, Part Three: Jesus Speaks to Sinners.

Jesus Speaks to Children
and
Mary Our Blessed Mother, Speaks to Children

These two illustrated childrens books contain messages
taken from *Volume Six*

The "Heaven Speaks" Booklets
as given to Anne, a lay apostle

Heaven Speaks About Abortion
Heaven Speaks About Addictions
Heaven Speaks to Victims of Clerical Abuse
Heaven Speaks to Consecrated Souls
Heaven Speaks About Depression
Heaven Speaks About Divorce
Heaven Speaks to Prisoners
Heaven Speaks to Soldiers
Heaven Speaks About Stress
Heaven Speaks to Young Adults
Heaven Speaks to Those Away from the Church
Heaven Speaks to Those Considering Suicide
Heaven Speaks to Those Who Do Not Know Jesus
Heaven Speaks to Those Who Are Dying
Heaven Speaks to Those Who Experience Tragedy
Heaven Speaks to Those Who Fear Purgatory
Heaven Speaks to Parents Who Worry
About Their Children's Salvation
Heaven Speaks to Those Who Have Rejected God
Heaven Speaks to Those Who Struggle to Forgive
Heaven Speaks to Those Who Suffer
from Financial Need

Heaven Speaks Collection
Contains all 20 Heaven Speaks booklets

The Big Books
Other Written Works by Anne, a lay apostle

Climbing the Mountain
Discovering Your Path to Holiness
Anne's experiences of Heaven

The Mist of Mercy
Spiritual Warfare and Purgatory
Anne's experiences of Purgatory

Serving in Clarity
A Guide for Apostles of the Returning King

Lessons in Love
Moving Toward Divine Intimacy

Whispers from the Cross
Reclaiming the Church through Personal Holiness

Transforming Grace
Becoming Thoughtful Men and Women of God

Staying in Place
Recovery in the Church

Suspended in Mystery
The Eucharist, Mary, and Mothers of the Church

**In Defense of Obedience
& Reflections on the Priesthood**

Excerpts from The Big Books

Purgatory, Prayer and Forgiveness
Excerpted from *The Mist of Mercy.*

Heaven
Excerpted from *Climbing the Mountain.*

**Thoughtful Men and Women of God.
A Guide to Contemplative Prayer.**
Excerpted from *Transforming Grace.*

Have you been blessed by reading this book?

Please help others receive these words by donating to Direction for Our Times. We are a registered 501(c)3 not for profit organization in the United States and all donations are tax deductible. In Ireland, we are a Registered Charity CHY17298.

We are a small organization with a big mission. Your donation makes all the difference. Monthly or one-time donations are gratefully accepted.

Headquarters in Ireland:
Tearmann Anama
Headquarters of The Apostolate of the Returning King
Ballyjamesduff, Co. Cavan, A82 Y670
Republic of Ireland
+353-(0)49-437-3040
contactus@dfot.ie
Registered Charity CHY17298

Office in the United States:
Direction For Our Times
9000 West 81st Street
Justice, Illinois 60458
USA
+1-708-496-9300
contactus@directionforourtimes.org
A 501(c)(3) Organization

To purchase these writings in either hard copy or electronically, please visit our website:
www.directionforourtimes.org

Have you ever wondered about Purgatory?

Do you expect to go there when you die?

In this video Anne describes her visions of Purgatory and the many beautiful realities of remorse, purification and love. She describes specific souls she encounters and explains their condition as we learn about the process of moving from anguish to peace when souls grasp the truth in greater and greater amounts. Taken from the book The Mist of Mercy, the discussion on the privacy of remorse, all alone, helps people to accept what is arguably God's greatest mercy. Viewers find this elegant film *"life changing"* and *"so calming"*. Anne, herself, would say *"Purgatory is like another word for Truth."*

This is a super film to share with family and friends.

"Experiencing this film will forever change your view of how God prepares souls for eternal joy in Heaven."

The movie Heaven adapted from the book *Climbing the Mountain.*

Based on the book *Climbing the Mountain* by Anne, a lay apostle, this movie explores one woman's mystical experience of Heaven. Through her encounters, Anne is shown the infinite grace, the laughter and love and creativity that awaits us in the heavenly kingdom upon completion of our earthly journey. This movie brings to life the landscapes, waters and healed and loving relationships described in *Climbing the Mountain* and reveals the lack of separation between Heaven and Earth.

Beautiful cinematography, combined with first person testimony, combines to make this film an unforgettable experience.

"A life changer. You'll go forward differently after seeing this film and encountering these concepts, which resonate."

Notes